Intimacy with
Christ Jesus

SUSIE ADWOA KOFFIE

Intimacy with Christ Jesus

© 2022 by Susie Adwoa Koffie

All rights reserved. No part of this book may be reproduced or transmitted in any form or by any means without written permission of the author.

Scripture quotations marked KJV are taken from the King James Version. Public Domain.

Scripture quotations marked NIV are taken from the New International Version Holy Bible, New International Version®, NIV® Copyright ©1973, 1978, 1984, 2011 by Biblica, Inc.® All rights reserved.

Scripture quotations marked NKJV are taken from the New King James Version ®. Copyright © 1982 by Thomas Nelson. All rights reserved.

Scripture quotations marked ESV are taken from the ESV Bible (The Holy Bible, English Standard Version®). Copyright © 2001 by Crossway Bibles, a publishing ministry of Good News Publishers. All rights reserved.

Scripture quotations marked The Voice (VOICE) are taken from The Voice Bible. Copyright © 2012 Thomas Nelson, Inc. The Voice™ translation © 2012 Ecclesia Bible Society All rights reserved.

Scripture quotations marked NLT are taken from the New Living Translation Holy Bible, New Living Translation, copyright © 1996, 2004, 2015 by Tyndale House Foundation. All rights reserved.

Published by:
Eleviv Publishing Group
10001 Dayton Lebanon Pike
Centerville, OH 45458
info@elevivpublishing.com
elevivpublishing.com
937-907-5001

ISBN: 978-1-952744-20-4 (paperback)

978-1-952744-37-2 (eBook)

Printed in the United States

5 4 3 2 1

Table of Contents

Dedication
Acknowledgment
Foreword
01: What is Intimacy? ...*pg10*
02: My Personal Encounter ...*pg15*
03: How to Develop a Personal and Intimate Relationship With God. ...*pg19*
04: An Effective Prayer Life. ...*pg21*
05: Benefits of Intimacy. ...*pg27*
06: Intimacy Killers ...*pg40*
07: Prayers That Bring Intimacy With Christ Jesus. ...*pg49*
08: Scripture on Intimacy With Christ Jesus. ...*pg54*
09: Connect and Stay With Jesus. ...*pg64*
10: Salvation Prayer. ...*pg66*

DEDICATION

This book is solely dedicated to the MOST-HIGH GOD who led me to write it and made everything possible. To Him ALONE be ALL the Glory, Honor and Adoration!!

To my entire family, I say a big thank you for all your support!
To my Wonderful & Precious Children,
Farida & Hakeem

You are my pride & joy!!
I thank the Almighty God for you guys every single second of everyday in my life.

The greatest blessings!
The greatest bundle of happiness!

I love you guys so much
With ALL & more of my heart FOREVER!!

Mummy/S.A.K

My Soul Thirsts for You
A Psalm of David when he was in the wilderness of Judah.

63 O God, you are my God; earnestly I seek you;
  my soul thirsts for you;
  my flesh faints for you,
as in a dry and weary land where there is no water.
² So I have looked upon you in the sanctuary,
  beholding your power and glory.
³ Because your steadfast love is better than life,
  my lips will praise you.
⁴ So I will bless you as long as I live;
  in your name I will lift up my hands.
⁵ My soul will be satisfied as with fat and rich food,
  and my mouth will praise you with joyful lips,
⁶ when I remember you upon my bed,
  and meditate on you in the watches of the night;
⁷ for you have been my help,
  and in the shadow of your wings I will sing for joy.
⁸ My soul clings to you;
  your right hand upholds me.

PSALM 63:1-8 (ESV)

FOREWORD

We are all created by God to fulfill purpose and destiny. How we achieve this goal can ONLY be attained by accepting Christ as our Lord and Personal Savior and having an intimate relationship with Him. Our Creator and our Maker, the Most-High God, created us to have a relationship with us. He wants to spend time with us and reveal Himself to us so that He can grant us divine direction for our lives. Living independently of God often leads us to a long, confusing, windy road. We fail, we falter, and we do it on our own, which often conflicts with God's purpose for our lives. Aligning God's will to our lives and understanding His plan and purpose for our lives puts us on the right path to fulfilling our destinies. Enquiring from God who to marry, what university to attend, what degree to pursue, what the right profession is, who to associate with as business partners, what friends we need to entangle with is an excellent step in the right direction to walking in the perfect will of God for our lives. Having a formidable intimate relationship with God and spending time in His word, praying and fasting, praising, and worshiping Him is the only way to find answers to all the questions we have into becoming who God wants us to be. A radical relationship with God starts with an intimate conversation devoid of distractions. Consistently being in His Presence, seeking answers through prayers, and quietly waiting for Him to speak back is the right step in the right direction for fulfilling our purpose here on earth. This book will walk you through how to create that intimate relationship with God and the benefits you will derive after forming that intimate relationship with Him. *'Draw near to God, and he will draw near to you.'* James 4:8a (ESV)

PLEASANT READING!

~**Susie Adwoa Koffie**

WHAT IS INTIMACY?

01

As born-again Christians, we must develop a deep, abiding, and intimate relationship with our Heavenly Father. The extent of intimacy we have with the Almighty God will determine how many victories and accomplishments we experience in our lives. An intimate relationship isn't automatically developed because you are born again. A close and deep relationship with God is available to every believer, but it must be nurtured, cultivated, and developed like any other relationship. If we do not pay attention, we can get caught up in the distinct roles we assume in our local churches that we will neglect the foundation principle of Christianity, which is our relationship with God. Our Heavenly Father wants to be involved in every area of our lives. He wants to communicate with us consistently. Therefore, it is vitally important that we do everything necessary to develop our relationship with God and deepen our levels of intimacy with Him. As we mature spiritually in our understanding of God's word and learn more about the fundamentals of His Kingdom, we must make sure that we do not get so busy focusing on working on all the fundamentals that we forget about our relationship with God. You can get absorbed in developing the fundamentals that you lose sight of the

Heavenly Father from whom those fundamentals originated. You can indulge yourself in the fundamentals of God's word and, all the while, not cultivate your relationship with Him. We always need to remember that at the beginning of every fundamental in the word of God, there is a Person with whom we are supposed to have a relationship. The fundamentals of God's word without an intimate relationship with Him is just a baseless religion. Without an intimate relationship with God, there will be no life in the fundamentals you apply. God is life, and without a relationship with Him, there will be no life in the fundamentals. You can get into a place where you have no relationship with God, and all that is left is just you and the fundamentals. That is why some of the fundamentals have become inactive in people's lives. The fundamentals of the word of God are vital to every believer. If the fundamentals of The Kingdom are not applied, the blessings of The Kingdom will not be experienced. However, those same fundamentals will become worrisome, lifeless, and void of power without an intimate relationship with God. To function with power, every fundamental must be applied in that relationship. God wants to have an intimate relationship with you and fellowship with you daily. In Revelation 3:20, Jesus says, *"Behold, I stand at the door, and knock: if any man hears my voice, and opens the door, I will come into him, and will sup with him, and he with me."* Jesus is indicating that He wants to fellowship with you. Also, 2 Corinthians 13:14 says, *"The grace of the Lord Jesus Christ, and the love of God, and the communion of the Holy Ghost, be with you all."* The word communion in that verse means fellowship or intimacy. According to the Bible, it is the will of God that we fellowship and have intimacy with the Spirit of God. God is always welcoming you to fellowship with Him. God is yearning to fellowship with you, talk with you, and be involved in every part of your life. The lack of success of many believers is that they embark on so many activities alone and never take God along with them. Irrespective of what activities you are engaged in, always make God a part of it. Practice His presence in everything that you do. Stay in constant communication with God. As 1 Chronicles 16:11 says, *"Seek the LORD and his strength, seek his face continually."* We should be talking to God and fellowshipping with Him continually, all the time, and in everything we do. Psalm 16:11 says, *"In your presence is fullness of joy."* When you are in constant fellowship with God, you will find that His very presence will bring joy to your every endeavor. The unfortunate thing for many believers is that they engage in spiritual activities without God. They are so consumed with prayer, speaking the word, studying it, and reading it that they forget to involve God in those things. We need to fellowship with God as we read, study, and pray. When God is involved, He will take your reading, studying, and praying to a deeper level than you could ever imagine. Your Heavenly Father desires to be heavily involved in your every activity. When God gets involved in your activities, He will inject them with heavenly joy and delight. That is what being saved is all about, having a personal relationship with your Heavenly Father and His Son Jesus. In John 17:3, Jesus said, *"And this is life eternal, that they might know you the only true God, and Jesus Christ, whom you have sent."* Jesus said eternal life is to know the Father and His Son Jesus Christ intimately. When you get born again, THE GREATEST asset gained is the new found ability to fellowship with the Father and His Son Jesus. That is eternal life. It is access back into the Father's presence to fellowship with Him.

One of the most incredible benefits you will gain from an intimate relationship with God is the ability to trust Him more EASILY. The more intimately you know someone (their character and their nature), the easier to trust them. In 2 Timothy 1:12, the Apostle Paul said, *"For I know whom I have believed, and am persuaded that he is able to keep that which I have committed unto him against that day."* The Apostle Paul intimately knew the God in whom he believed. It is extremely difficult to trust somebody you do not know. While on the other hand, the better you know someone, the easier it is for you to trust them. For example, if you had to leave your child with a stranger on the street versus your best friend, it would be much easier to trust your best friend simply because you know them better. Now, that stranger could be a person of higher character and integrity than your best friend. Your child could even be in better hands with that stranger than with your best friend, but your ability to trust them is thwarted because you do not know them. When your RELATIONSHIP with God is no longer being developed, your faith in God cannot grow. Relationship growth is hard where an intimate relationship is not present.

Romans 10:17 says, *"So then faith comes by hearing and hearing by the Word of God."* Many have taken that verse and made it all principle and no relationship. Like spiritual robots, they spend much time in the word only to never have their faith developed to where they know it should be. The development of your faith is not only about *"spending time in the word,"* it is about spending time with God and getting to know Him more intimately, and you do that by spending time in His word. The word of God indeed contains the faith of God. As you spend time in the word of God, your faith in God will get stronger. However, if you spend time in the word of God religiously, not being conscious of your relationship with God, your faith will never reach the heights it should go. Faith does come by hearing the word, but it also comes as your relationship with God deepens. As you spend time in the word of God, the faith contained in that word will ultimately begin to fill your heart. The other piece to growing your faith is that as you spend time in the word of God, you are spending time with God and getting to know Him better. The better you know Him, the easier it is for you to trust Him.

MY PERSONAL ENCOUNTER — 02

I went to church all my life but had no relationship with Christ Jesus. I would wake up, say a quick prayer, and read a quick devotional, but I was never deep in the things of God. I thought people were doing too much and were very excessive with the things I heard them doing concerning their spiritual lives. I was born a Presbyterian and went to Presbyterian churches in my younger years. I started occasionally going to a few Pentecostal churches till I relocated to the United States. I started going to a Baptist Church, and I loved it because it was a simple service with no complications. Even when I moved away to a new location, I found another Baptist church, and I loved it because it was void of drama and was primarily Caucasian and a few Black people when I started. The Pastor was white and very loving, and I was like, yes, no drama and just an hour-long service from 11 A.M. to 12 noon. That meant that I only spent an hour with the Lord in a whole week. I was in that church for over twelve years: no spiritual growth and no depth in the things of God. I was the Prayer Chain lead, taught the children's church, and handled church announcements via email.

Meanwhile, I felt an emptiness and knew something was

missing in my life. As I began to reflect on my life and noticed certain things were not in alignment, I realized something was missing in my life. Around that same time, my friend invited me to a prayer line, and I agreed to join, and my life has never been the same.

Oh, My Goodness!! The word of God was taught in-depth, and prayers were said in a way I had never felt before. For the first time in my life, I would pick up my Bible and would not put it down. I grew more inquisitive, and I wanted to know more about Jesus. I would wake up in the early morning hours with my Bible, reading and seeking to learn more. I accepted Jesus Christ as my Lord and Personal Savior, and I decided to follow Him for the rest of my life. I gradually began to see massive changes in my life. My love for TV suddenly grew cold.

I stopped watching the news, which was unbelievable since I loved politics and always wanted "to be in the know." I started listening to Christian channels and teachings. I would write down scriptures and research anything that I did not understand. I became deeply involved in the things of God. I prayed more, studied my Bible more, and loved to worship in my car. On my way back and forth to work, I would always communicate with God through worship or prayer. Then I started dreaming, and God started talking to me and revealing deep and secret things to me. I was overwhelmed and realized that these were really some good encounters, and now everything became so real. God would reveal so many things to me about people around me, and they would confirm it. The divine visitations became constant, and I knew the hand of God was truly on me. I was no longer interested in engaging in unnecessary long phone calls and being in places and environments that would make me drift away from the presence of the Lord. I could not have enough of this new found love. I figured the more I stayed in His presence and spent more quality time with Him, the more I heard from Him. I noticed that I could not join in certain conversations.

I would immediately go back to God for forgiveness anytime I had a conversation that was out of line or when I did anything that did not Glorify the name of the Lord or grieve the Holy Spirit that was residing in me because I had accepted Jesus Christ as my Lord and Savior. My spirit would grieve for things I would say, and I felt the Holy Spirit in me so much. My prayer life kept growing, and my love for the Bible became very eminent. I loved the Psalms because they were very comforting, and I could use them to pray. I started memorizing scriptures, especially the Psalms, since they just became too real to me. I loved my new life and loved hearing the voice of God.

Things started making sense to me, and the emptiness completely left. I would worship for hours because the presence I felt in worship was something else. The Lord opened my eyes, and I thanked the Lord for saving me at the time He did. Sometimes I would ask Him, Father, why did you not call me earlier? Because I had made many wrong choices that had caused me so much. I was asking Him that

Father if I had a closer relationship with you and heard from you, I would never have made certain decisions and choices, but the Lord kept assuring me that He makes all things beautiful in His own time. As I grew in the Lord and continued to seek him daily, I started receiving scriptures in my dreams. I would wake up and write them down, and I knew I had found my best friend ever and the love of my life. He heard my silent prayers and appeared to me in my dreams, assuring me never to fear because He was always with me and took me through some of the darkest days. I love you so much, Jesus. Thank you for dying on the cross for me. Thank you for shedding your blood. Thank you for giving me this opportunity to know you truly. Where would I have been without you? Thank you for making me write this book and share with the world the benefits of having a great and intimate relationship with you. Thank you for everything.

I would not be alive today without you. You have been my Pillar and My Rock. My very portion in the Land of the Living. I was led to write this book to share my experience with regular people like me who have been in church all their lives but never had a personal relationship with Christ Jesus. You can be going to church every day and serving distinct roles in the church, but you do not have a relationship with your Maker. God created us to have a deep and abiding relationship with Him. He cares for you to serve in the church and take a role as an assignment in church, but that should not take away the time you spend with your Heavenly Father.

HOW TO DEVELOP A PERSONAL AND INTIMATE RELATIONSHIP WITH GOD

03

So now, what is this personal relationship, and how do we acquire this?

First is a genuine acceptance of Christ Jesus as your Lord and personal Savior. Say this prayer aloud right now:

"Dear God, I want to be a part of your family. I know that I am a sinner, and I ask for Your forgiveness. You said in Your Word that if I acknowledge that You raised Jesus from the dead and accept Him as my Lord and Saviour, I would be saved. So, God, I now say that I believe You raised Jesus from the dead and that He is alive and well. I accept Him now as my Personal Lord and Savior. I accept my salvation from sin right now.

I am now saved! Jesus is my Lord and my Savior. Thank you, Father God, for forgiving me, saving me, and giving me eternal life with You. Amen!" (Romans 10:9-10).

Second is the development of your faith. How do you develop your faith?

1. Read your Bible daily

2. Meditate on the word of God

3. Set a time and place to pray daily

4. Love the Lord with all your heart

5. Be obedient to His word

6. Trust the Lord with all your heart

7. Fast regularly as the spirit leads

8. Worship and Praise Him always

9. Listen to Christian messages

10. Let the Holy Spirit of the Lord lead you

11. Increase your giving and take care of widows, orphans, the poor, and the needy.

12. Evangelize and win souls for Christ.

AN EFFECTIVE PRAYER LIFE

04

Daily Prayers

The Presence of God: - Father, I thank you for the gift of life and the grace to see a new day. Let your presence go into this day's journey with my family and me. It is written in Exodus 33:14 (ESV), *"And he said, My presence will go with you, and I will give you rest."* Grant me and my family rest, and let your presence NEVER depart from us in the Mighty Name of Jesus. Amen!!

The Provision of God: - Father, as I go into this day with my family, provide us ALL our needs according to Your riches in glory in Christ Jesus. It is written in Psalm 23:1 that *"The Lord is My Shepherd; I shall not want."* My family and I will never lack any good thing in the Mighty Name of Jesus.

The Protection & Preservation of God: - Father, preserve and protect my going out and my coming in, in the Mighty Name of Jesus. I pray for journey mercies for myself and my family. Protect us this day. I cancel any evil dream, and I pray against any evil plan, plot, scheme, or device of the wicked assigned against me and my family this day in the Mighty Name of Jesus. Declare Psalms 121, 91, and 27.

The Peace of God: - Let the Peace of God that surpasses ALL understanding be my portion and that of my spouse, children, and the entire family as we journey into this day and the remaining days of this year in the Mighty Name of Jesus. (Philippians 4:6-7)

The Power & Fire of God: - Father, let my spirit, my soul, and my body and that of my family become fire and power so that no power nor principality shall have access to any part of our lives in your Mighty Name. Let our lives and destinies become untouchable by any force of darkness in Jesus' Mighty Name.

Commit the day into the hands of God: - Father Lord, I commit this new day into your Mighty Hands. Order my steps and that of my family according to your will. Father, cause us to always be at the right place at the right time. Go ahead of us and make every crooked path straight in the Name of Jesus. Jeremiah 10:23, Psalm 37:23, and Isaiah 45:2.

Plead the Blood of Jesus: - Father Lord, I plead the blood of Jesus over my spirit, my soul, and my body. I soak my family in the blood of Jesus. I soak my house from the roofing to the foundation in the blood of Jesus. I soak the work of my hands in the blood of Jesus. I soak my car and my journey this day in your precious blood. Let your blood be a mark of protection and immunity over my life and my family in the Mighty Name of Jesus.

Have a list of people on your prayer list: - Pray for them daily. Mention their names individually and pray for them for Heaven to register their names. Do this daily at your devotion and your prayer time. *"First of all, then, I urge that supplications, prayers, intercessions, and thanksgiving be made for all people."* 1 Timothy 2:1 (ESV)

Pray for your church and the body of Christ: - Father, you have built your church, and the gates of hell shall never prevail against it. Fight for your church and deliver your church and the body of Christ from the hands of the wicked. Matthew 16:17-19 (ESV)

Pray for the leaders: - Remember to pray for the leaders of your country both at home and wherever you have settled, community, church, and your place of work. *"I urge, then, first of all, that petitions, prayers, intercession, and thanksgiving be made for all people --for kings and all those in authority, that we may live peaceful and quiet lives in all godliness and holiness."* (1 Timothy 2:1-2).

Pray for the five-fold Ministry: - Pray for the Apostles, the Evangelists, the Prophets, the Pastors, and the teachers that God has blessed us with this end time.

Attend Seasonal Retreats: - Take time out of your busy schedule and seek God to transform and rejuvenate your spiritual life.

Attend Holy-Sprit-filled events: – Do not forsake the assembly of the brethren, so partake in programs at your church or other Spirit-filled churches you are invited to. Always pray about any invitation that you get. Beware of false prophets and churches. The Bible declares that we test every spirit. (1 John 4:1)

Have a Consistent Prayer & Fasting Life: - Always pray and make it a habit to pray at midnight for difficult situations. A consistent and aggressive prayer life will always yield remarkable results. (1 Thessalonians 5:17). Fast regularly and seek God's face since fasting will benefit you immensely in your spiritual journey and walk with Christ Jesus. (Isaiah 58:8-16).

Trust in the Lord with all your heart: - Put all your trust in the Almighty God. Not some of your trust, but ALL of it. It is the God that you have come to know whose spirit dwells in you. For with God, the Bible declares that ALL things are POSSIBLE. Do not manipulate situations in your own strength. As you pray to God, believe wholeheartedly that He will see you through no matter what. (Proverbs 3:5-6).

Always obey the Lord: - As you receive directions and instructions from God, quickly be obedient and do as the Lord says. Do not keep asking friends for confirmation as you have clearly heard from God. Consistent disobedience from God will block you from hearing from Him. The Bible declares that if you love God, you will keep His commandments which depicts total obedience to His word. (John 14:15)

Total dependence on the Holy Spirit: - Be sensitive to the Holy Spirit. The Holy Spirit is our Helper, Teacher, Guide, Leader, and Advocate. He makes our prayers effective, makes the scriptures come alive, and speaks to our hearts. The Holy Spirit empowers us to overcome spiritual opposition to the preaching of the gospel and God's work in people's lives.

The Spirit of God also gives us discernment in situations of spiritual conflict against the forces of darkness. (Romans 8:9).

Be a Faithful Giver: - Pay your tithe, which is 10% of your total salary, sow seeds, remember orphans, widows, and the poor. Be in a consistent giving plan and help and support your local church. *"Each one must give as he has decided in his heart, not reluctantly or under compulsion, for God loves a cheerful giver."* (2 Corinthians 9:7 ESV). *"Bring the full tithe into the storehouse, that there may be food in my house. And thereby put me to the test, says the Lord of hosts, if I will not open the windows of heaven for you and pour down for you a blessing until there is no more need."* (Malachi 3:10 ESV)

Forgive: - The Bible teaches us that we should forgive those who trespass against us. The Bible says to be merciful as your Father is also merciful. Forgiveness frees your spirit. When the Apostle Peter asked Jesus, *"Lord, how often shall my brother sin against me, and I forgive him, till seven times? Jesus saith unto him, I say not unto thee, Until seven times: but, until seventy times seven."* (Matt 18:21-22). Jesus was not telling Peter to forgive someone 490 times and stop at 491. Rather, the numbers Jesus used were symbolic of infinity. We must forgive unconditionally and infinitely.

Runaway from sin: - Flee from fornication, rebellion, sexual immorality, impurity, sensuality, idolatry, sorcery, enmity, strife, jealousy, fits of anger, rivalries, dissensions, divisions, envy, and drunkenness. (Colossians 3:5 ESV)

Flow in the Gifts of the Spirit: - *"To each is given the* *manifestation of the Spirit for the common good. For to one is given through the Spirit the utterance of wisdom, and to another the utterance of knowledge according to the same Spirit, to another faith by the same Spirit, to another gifts of healing by the one Spirit, to another the working of miracles, to another prophecy, to another the ability to distinguish between spirits, to another various kinds of tongues, to another the interpretation of tongues. All these are empowered by one and the same Spirit, who apportions to each one individually as he wills."* (1 Corinthians 12:7-11 ESV)

Flow in the Fruit of the Spirit: – *"But the fruit of the Spirit is love, joy, peace, patience, kindness, goodness, faithfulness, gentleness, self-control; against such things there is no law."* (Galatians 5:22-23 (ESV)

Be of service at your local church: - Use your talents and your God-given gifts to serve the Lord in His House.

BENEFITS OF INTIMACY — 05

Intimacy brings God's absolute best into our lives. Through the journey of developing an intimate relationship with God, we can hear from God and walk in His perfect will for our lives. Anytime we read our Bible and study the word, the Lord speaks to us and reveals deep and secret things to us. Anytime we pray and listen to Him after prayer, we hear from Him. God is very attentive to every detail and circumstance of our lives. He captures even the trivial things that escape our notice. The Lord loves us so much that He cares about the problems, burdens, directions, and decisions that concern us in our relationship with Him. Remember, our God is a Planner, and He even knew us before we were formed. (Jeremiah 1:5) I have learned that we tend to put God first in our lives when we have an intimate relationship with Him.

Spending time with God becomes a vital necessity in our lives. We can do what we are called to do because we are in the presence of God every day, seeking His face. We realize that if we do not have time for God first, nothing in our lives will work. God is not happy with second place or third place in our lives. We turn the telephone off, say no to our friends, turn away from all distractions and seek Him. This is when our relationship with Him grows deeper, knowing that He is the first place in our lives. When you build a close relationship with God, you see things through His eyes. It is a bond forged in love and nurtured through continual communication and trust. By stepping back and putting your complete faith in God and the outcome of all your affairs, you invite God into your life with loving trust and friendship. As your relationship deepens, you begin to see how God truly does oversee your growth as a soul and how he steers your course as you navigate your way through this lifetime.

This is a win-win situation! The Almighty God already knows your goals and what you are to accomplish while here on earth. That was carefully planned with your consent before you were born on this Earth. Your destiny includes a series of events that define the lessons that you are to learn. How you accomplish them, and if you do, is entirely up to you. Awareness of your divine assignment, as well as the knowledge that you have gained from a multitude of lifetimes, is masked by the ego when you are born. One of the tasks that we have as a spiritual being on a human journey is to break through the veil that appears to separate us from that knowledge and the universal truths accessible through communication. As you develop your relationship with God, your trust and faith are rewarded with spiritual strength, love, knowledge, and peace. The word of God becomes strongly alive in you.

As a result, you find yourself emulating the very characteristics that God displays toward you through His word, including a significant capacity to extend love, forgiveness, understanding, and compassion toward yourself and others. Intimacy with Christ guarantees that you are not alone on your journey. Christ is always with you as He has promised us that He will always be with us till the end of time. (Matthew 28:20) That is you who have accepted Christ and yielded fully to Him. God is there to oversee and lovingly direct your path. The best way to hear Him is to invite Him into your life. Speak with Him, pray to Him and with Him, share your thoughts and your gratitude, ask for guidance, and be open to His answers. God resides within you. He does not punish you with seemingly negative situations. Some circumstances are part of what God has destined, while others are the result of how we treat ourselves and others.

Negative thoughts and actions ripple across the earth, causing reactions and events directly affecting our lives. God sees this happening. He intervenes when it is appropriate for him to do so. There are times when lessons are needed to be learned. At those times, it may seem as though He is not listening or punishing you with hurtful or painful situations. You might even ask: *"Why should I be the one going through this experience?"* He may not be removing you from it because, if he did, it may hamper your growth and hurt you more in the long run. When you need assistance, call on God to help you get through the tough situations you face and be open to his guidance. The angels are there for you, too. Calm the fears within yourself by embracing the love of God and know that He will ensure the best outcome for you. It may not be the outcome you had hoped and prayed for, but then again, maybe it will.

Remain still and feel the peace within your heart that is given with grace to you by God. His love always flows through your being. When you remain calm through any demanding situation, you can feel God's love in its purest form. It is a glorious feeling of unspeakable joy, almost overwhelming in its power. When you experience it, you will know that it is sent to you directly from God. We walk in wisdom when we have an intimate and abiding relationship with the Almighty God. We are not just able to live our lives anyhow. Remember the Spirit of the Lord resides in us. That same spirit that rose Jesus from the dead lives in us. The Holy Spirit is our teacher and teaches us where to go and gives us the wisdom to make the right choices and decisions if we are overly sensitive to the voice of God. We encounter God's amazing promises when we completely depend on Him.

Many people deal with anxiety. News reports or circumstances at home often cause concern and fear about our future. But as believers who have an intimate relationship with God, we are encouraged not to worry (Luke 12:22). Instead, we are to seek God's kingdom and rely on Him to provide for all our needs (Luke 12:31). This is the opposite of the world's philosophy and to those who do not know Christ or have an intimate relationship with Him, which tells us to rely on ourselves or other people for security. We can confidently depend on our Heavenly Father because He

Himself is the truth (John 14:6), and His promises are true. According to Titus 1:2, God cannot lie and never makes a promise that He will not keep. And He certainly, has the power to keep His word, for *"nothing will be impossible with God"* (Luke 1:37).

The Lord is also mindful of all our needs. Looking at His excellent provision for birds and flowers, we can be confident of His even greater care for His beloved children. What a relief to know our Heavenly Father is both intimately acquainted with our needs and eager to meet them. The difference for us who know Christ is that we believe in God, seek His kingdom, and rest in His peace that surpasses understanding (Phil. 4:7). We make prayer a priority when Christ becomes our focus. It is prayer that grows the deep relationship. We are told to *"pray without ceasing"* in the Bible (1 Thessalonians 5:17). While God does not expect us to go through life muttering prayers under our breath, we are called to be ever mindful of Him and quick to offer our petitions, praise, and gratitude throughout the day.

And this will become a reality only when we make prayer a daily priority by setting aside time to be alone with the Lord, reading His Word, and talking to Him. The purpose is not simply to bring Him a list of requests before quickly heading out the door. Any good relationship requires time and two-way communication. The goal is to have a conversation with God as we read His word and respond in prayer. When this becomes a habit, our thoughts will quickly and regularly turn to God in dependence, thankfulness, and worship. Anytime you notice a shift in your prayer life, ask the Lord for His help quickly. Realize, however, that a consistent habit of prayer will also require diligence on your part. You may have to get up earlier, but any sacrifice will be worth the effort because the outcome will be an intimate, satisfying relationship with your loving heavenly Father.

Time is a most valuable commodity. Since it is irreversible and irreplaceable, we ought to give careful consideration to how we spend our days and even our minutes. Time is a gift from God, which means we are not owners but stewards who will one day give an account for how we used what was entrusted to us (Ephesians 5:7-17). Those who have a deep relationship with God realize their days belong to God, and they are cautious about how they live. They want to understand the Lord's will and seek His guidance each day through intimate fellowship with Him in His word and prayer. But those who do not have a relationship with God do not give adequate thought to the way they live. Some become unproductive and lazy, living for their own pleasures. But even those who are busy and successful by worldly standards may be wasting their time if their schedules are not aligned with God's will.

To make the most of your opportunities, try beginning each day with the Lord, asking Him to direct your activities. None of us want to arrive in heaven and discover that although we have been busy spending our time, we have failed to invest in eternity. Clinging to hope is difficult when we do not have a relationship with Christ. Circumstances are miserable and show no signs of improving. This can be incredibly discouraging when we know that our all-powerful God could remedy the situation and fulfill our dreams but has not. Hope is essential for life in a fallen world. Unless we believe something better awaits us in the future, we might sink into utter despair. But optimistic anticipation can also bring disappointment when we look forward to something that does not materialize.

Hope is secure when it is aligned with the Lord's desires, revealed in scripture. However, many of our expectations are based on wishes or feelings. We long for things like job promotions, good health, strong relationships, or quick solutions to our problems, but the Lord has no absolute promise that these are part of His will for us. Disappointment with God can occur whenever our expectations do not coincide with His plan because we do not have a deep and abiding relationship with Him. Even when hope is based on a scriptural promise, the Lord may not fulfill it in the way or the timeframe that we expect. Contentment lies in distinguishing subjective hopes, which originate with us, from our ultimate hope in the Lord, who is Sovereign and Good. Then, even when an earthly expectation isn't met as we wished, we can have joy, remembering that our eternal hope in God is sure. It is God's character to reveal His will to you who have an intimate relationship with Him.

If the Lord wants you to live a certain way and make specific choices, He must assume responsibility for teaching you the right thing to do. He understands that the road can become confusing and that often the choices we face are difficult and complex. But as a good and faithful Father who sees what is ahead, He is more than willing to help us. He says so many times in His Word. In Psalm 32:8, He assures us, *"I will instruct you and teach you in the way which you should go; I will counsel you with my eye upon you."* This is why you read about people such as David praying, *"Teach me to do Your will, for You are my God; let Your good Spirit lead me on level ground"* (Psalm 143:10). David knew that it was (and still is) the Lord's character to want us to know what His will is so that we may walk in it (1 Chronicles 16:8–12). God also promises that He will show you His will. James 1:5 proclaims, *"If any of you lacks wisdom, let him ask of God, who gives to all generously and without reproach, and it will be given to him."* Likewise, (Proverbs 28:5) affirms, *"Those who seek the Lord understand all things."*

In fact, throughout the Bible, you will find numerous promises the Father has given to reveal His plans to you. So, in your walk with Him, let there be no doubt from this point forward. You can be confident the Lord will show you, His will. And if doubts do arise, place your rest in the assertion of Psalm 16:11: *"You will make known to me the path of life; in Your presence is fullness of joy; in Your right hand there are pleasures forever."* Jesus tells us that God's kingdom and righteousness should be our highest aim. God's kingdom must be pursued every day, moment by moment. This can only be achieved with total dependence on the Almighty God through a relationship with Him.

To seek the Father's kingdom is to submit to His rule over

every area of our lives. The bottom line is obedience. To seek God's righteousness means cooperating with His process of transforming us into Jesus' image. An integral part of this process is renewing our minds with scripture. The word of God keeps the Father's viewpoint and instructions fresh in our thinking. Your relationship with the Lord dominates your thoughts and affections. Where do you invest time and money? What desires govern your choices? Making Christ a top priority requires submission to God, obedience to His Word, and trust in His ways. And He promises to supply whatever you need in pursuing that goal (Phil. 4:19). True and inner peace only comes from an intimate relationship with Christ. Peace with God is a gift and not a reward. Every person who is right with God has been brought back into a peaceful relationship with him. It is the effect of something that God does.

Peace comes when you are truly born again and begin to have that deep relationship with God. Without the cross, we are nothing; therefore, being justified by faith, we have peace with Jesus. A life of peace, quietness, and tranquility from within can only be found in Jesus Christ. There is no substitute for INTIMACY with GOD. Do you know why you were created? You were created to have a close intimate relationship with God. This relationship makes us live a holy life. Informing this relationship, our life brings glory to Him. We also have the real security of being with Him after our time here on earth. Spending time with the Lord always quietens our spirit, grants us renewed energy, and strengthens our faith. We get to know the Lord and what He likes and dislikes. We are assured of answers to our prayers and a sense of direction. Our emotions are refreshed, and our views of the Lord get enlarged.

The Lord consistently speaks to our hearts, purifies our hearts, gives us insight and instruction, and we become addicted to studying God's word. Through studying His Word, we are made aware that we will go through afflictions, but the Lord will be with us to strengthen us. Therefore, an intimate relationship with our Lord and Saviour prepares us for unexpected conflicts. The one priority in our lives is our intimate relationship with Him. The story of Martha and Mary in Luke 10:38-42 depicts this. Intimacy with God is the quickest and surest way to receive God's power, authority, anointing, and grace to operate in our world. When you have a deep and abiding relationship with God, your enemies will become God's enemies, and they will succumb to His presence and power, which are evident in your life. His Spirit will dominate you and do wonders through you.

Becoming overly sensitive to the Spirit benefits us when we accept Christ as our Lord and Personal Savior, and we foster a relationship with Him. The Holy Spirit comes and dwells within us. The Holy Spirit is Our Counsellor because He gives us wise advice when we need it. He is also Our Comforter because before Jesus was crucified, He promised His followers that the Father would send them the Comforter, or the Holy Spirit (John 14:26–27). One benefit of the Holy Spirit is to offer comfort and peace. The Spirit comforts us when we are scared, lonely, or overwhelmed and fills us with "hope and perfect love." The Holy Spirit can guide us throughout our lives. As we prayerfully ask God for help, His Holy Spirit will show us all things we should do. One of the ways God communicates with us is through the Holy Spirit.

The Holy Spirit speaks to our minds and hearts through thoughts and feelings. Our Helper, our Intercessor who puts things on our minds to pray. He is our Advocate, our Lawyer, and our Strengthener. He is our Teacher who guides us into all truth and brings things into our remembrance. The Holy Spirit can help us to know the truth of all things. He testifies of the Heavenly Father and of Jesus Christ, as well as Jesus's divine role, God's love, and all other eternal truths. You can feel the Holy Spirit and confirm the truth in your heart and mind as you study the scriptures and pray for understanding. When we forget our dreams, and we call on the Holy Spirit to remind us, He does (Ephesians 3:16). The Holy Spirit convicts us of sin and lets us know what we are doing wrong. The Holy Spirit can change and purify your heart. We each experience internal, invisible struggles, and we may feel anger, hurt, or any other hard feelings caused by any number of circumstances.

Through our faith in Jesus, the Holy Spirit can cleanse our hearts and change our dispositions. It can help us forgive others, replace anger with love, and become more like Jesus. He will prompt us when we start to engage in gossip. The Holy Spirit brings the fulness of God when you accept Christ. He represents God in your life. He is there to connect your mind to the throne of God so that you can have access to divine information and knowledge. When we fall so deeply in love with Jesus, we will obey Him. The more we fall in love with Jesus, the more we draw close to Him and walk according to His will. The longer you abide in Christ and the deeper you go with Him, the more His presence permeates your life (John 15:5). Without Christ, who is the Vine, the strongest branch is as defenseless as the weakest branch. Studying God's word and obeying His word draws you closer to Him. The closer you get to God, the more you want to do what He says. You will begin to walk in His blessing. We truly need the power of the Holy Spirit to surrender and obey God in all areas of our lives. The Spirit of the Lord changes our hearts, so we have a tender-loving, responsive heart towards God. *"And I will give you a new heart, and I will put a new spirit in you. I will take out your stony, stubborn heart and give you a tender, responsive heart. And I will put my Spirit in you so that you will follow my decrees and be careful to obey my regulations."* Ezekiel 36:26-27.

The Holy Spirit helps you pray more effectively. *"In the same way, the Spirit helps us in our weakness. We do not know what we ought to pray for, but the Spirit himself intercedes for us through wordless groans"* (Romans 8:26 NIV). The Spirit of the Lord is a very much-needed prayer partner in the life of every believer. He knows the will of God, and He is always ready to help you pray anytime and anywhere.

"Very truly I tell you, whoever believes in me will do the works I have been doing, and they will do even greater things than these because

I am going to the Father." (John 14:12 NIV).

The Holy Spirit, who is our Helper, enables us to operate in the works of Jesus. This is only possible because we dwell under the influence. This spirit-filled experience is life-changing, and it reveals the healing and deliverance power of God. We benefit from the Holy Spirit as believers because the anointing flows through us to enable us to function in our God-given gifts and assignments, making it easy to fulfill our purpose here on earth.

When the Holy Spirit comes to dwell in us, we can embark on the commission that Jesus gives us to be witnesses of His word worldwide. "But you will receive power when the Holy Spirit comes on you; and you will be my witnesses in Jerusalem, and in all Judea and Samaria, and to the ends of the earth" (Acts 1:8NIV). That raw power to go and make disciples of all nations and teach them to obey all the Lord's commandments becomes easy to achieve. The Holy Spirit enables you to love more deeply. "And hope does not put us to shame, because God's love has been poured out into our hearts through the Holy Spirit, who has been given to us." (Romans 5:5). Jesus said that we should love above all.

Loving like Jesus cannot be achieved by our carnal flesh. It only flows into our hearts by the Holy Spirit. Only a Spirit-filled Believer can ignite the spiritual passion for loving God and people. Without the indwelling of the Holy Spirit, developing that rich, loving, deep, and intimate relationship with Christ Jesus becomes impossible. Therefore, the Holy Spirit plays an integral role in our relationship with the Lord.

A close and intimate relationship with God causes us to act very tactfully. Because we spend a lot of time in God's presence and read His word, our conversations will always be gracious and attractive (Colossians 4:6 NLT). We can deal with others tactfully. Exhibiting graciousness comes a little easier for those filled with the Spirit of the Lord. Since our goal is to be Christ-like, we tend to follow Jesus, who never allowed courtesy and kindness to stop Him from telling the truth. Jesus never did this in a mean-spirited way, and nor should we who are following Him and have developed a close relationship with Him. Intimacy helps the Believer develop the emotional discipline needed to deal with tactless remarks. You begin to walk in victory as you develop that relationship with God. You can manage every situation knowing that you are more than a conqueror. You start to live in dominion over sickness, disease, poverty, and lack. You receive good health, peace, prosperity, and success in all areas of your life because of that intimate relationship and your obedience to His word.

INTIMACY KILLERS — 06

There are a lot of distractions in our day to keep us from focusing on the Lord. After we have had our quiet time in the morning, which includes worshiping the Lord, reading the Bible, praying, and waiting to hear from the Lord before we start our day, we should keep meditating on the word that we have read ALL day. Even as we are working, we should keep the Lord in our hearts. Distractions like our personal phones, social media, which includes Facebook, WhatsApp, Instagram, Twitter, Texting, and all the numerous distractions should be in moderation. If you are using Facebook as a place to listen to messages and share the word of God, that is fine. Anything done excessively to take us away from our time with God is unhealthy. Also, unnecessarily long conversations on the phone, which always lead to some form of gossip, or the other is not pleasing in the sight of the Lord. There is nothing wrong with touching base with our children, spouses, family members, loved ones, and close friends but again, let all be done in moderation, not taking time away from the Lord. Excessive sleep, laziness, and procrastination should also be avoided. We must consistently stay focused on the Lord, our family, and the work of our hands. Giving more time in our day to meditate on the word of the Lord and share Jesus Christ as much as possible. Especially as we fast and pray and seek the face of the Lord, our focus should solely be on the Lord. Distractions in our day with unnecessary phone calls and social media interference take us away from our very purpose of going on a fast to seek the face of the Lord. The Bible declares that in confidence and in quietness lies your strength (Isaiah 30:15). When we are quiet, the Lord can speak to us so we can hear Him. We are in tune with His voice, and we yield so obediently to His voice. Life can be very draining and demanding, and the fact that you are a child of God does not mean you should allow the drainers to keep you from your focus which is the Lord. Initially, those around you may not like that you are spending more time with the Lord. Eventually, they will come to terms with it when they see you are disciplined and focused on the Lord. And at the end of the day, remember we will give an account of our lives and how we spent our time here on earth. Our accountability will be to our Heavenly Father and NOT to any man. The Bible says that owe no man anything except LOVE. Once you are not holding anything against anyone and just spending more time with God and working on your salvation with fear and trembling, you are in a good place. Knowingly living in sin will drive you away from the presence of the Lord. We feel guilty when sinning, which keeps us from effectively praying and spending time with God. Pride, self-elevation, self-importance, and seeking worldly importance will break our communication and intimate relationship with Christ. Pride always comes before a fall, and God opposes the proud. Pride is a sin, and it is a self-centered, rather than God-centered, perspective on life. We often find ourselves inordinately proud of our accomplishments and who we are. In turn, we do not give thanks to the Lord, our true source of strength. He is the one who gave us these abilities and opportunities, and all for the purpose of growing His kingdom. But he gives more grace. Therefore, His Word says, *"God opposes the proud but gives grace to the humble."* (James 4:6). Every believer should guard against seeking self and worldly importance. Human desires are part of God's creation and therefore not inherently evil, but they become twisted when not directed by and toward God. *"Not that we dare to classify or compare ourselves with some of those who are commending themselves. But when they measure themselves by one another and compare themselves with one another, they are without understanding."* (2 Corinthians 10:12). When people begin to put their security in the wealth they have acquired and totally boast in their riches, they take the Glory from God and begin to think they do not need God because they can make it on their own. The riches can give a false sense of security and break complete relationship from God. Pride completely separates us from God. Pride always exalts self above God. Pride kills your love for God, kills your passion for God, and kills your desire for God. Pride is behind every sin ever committed, every rebellion against God and His Word, and every fall of the heart of a person from the loving embrace of His Creator. Prayerlessness breaks our communication and intimacy with Christ. The quickest way to gain intimacy is our communication with Christ. Spending more time with the people we know, and love causes intimacy and that is the same with our relationship with Christ. The Bible instructs us to pray without ceasing so when we break that communion with Christ, we have sinned and lost that relationship that Christ so desires to have with us. Prayer connects us to God, prayer is an active way to love and connect with others, and prayer makes room in the believer's heart for God's correcting voice. The Bible says to *"pray continually"* (1 Thessalonians 5:17), so anything other than a continual attitude of prayer and communion with God is a sin. Anything that interrupts our connection to God or leads to self-reliance is wrong. Can you imagine someone claiming to be your best friend and never talking to you? Whatever friendship was, there would certainly be strained. Similarly, a relationship with God is impoverished and fatigued without communication. Prayerlessness is contrary to a good relationship with God. God's people will have a natural desire to communicate with their Lord. "In the morning, Lord, you hear my voice; in the morning, I lay my requests before you and wait expectantly" (Psalm 5:3). The biblical commands to pray are accompanied by wonderful promises: *"The LORD is near to all who call on him, to all who call on him in truth"* (Psalm 145:18).

Christ is our best example of prayerfulness. He Himself was a man of prayer (Luke 3:21; 5:16; 9:18, 28; 11:1), and He taught His followers to pray (Luke 11:2–4). If the Son of Man saw a personal need to pray, how much more should we see the same need in ourselves. Prayerlessness ignores the gift of intercession that God has given us. We are called to pray for our brothers and sisters in Christ (James 5:16). Paul often solicited the prayers of God's people on his behalf. (Ephesians 6:19; 1 Thessalonians 5:25; Colossians 4:3), and he was faithful to pray for them (Ephesians 1:16;

Colossians 1:9). The prophet Samuel saw prayers on behalf of the people of Israel as a necessary part of his ministry: *"As for me, far be it from me that I should sin against the LORD by failing to pray for you"* (1 Samuel 12:23). According to Samuel, prayerlessness is a sin. Fixing our eyes on Pastors, Prophets, Men of God, and Women of God and working to please them solely is an intimacy killer. Most of the time, we take positions in the church to please the Pastors that we serve. We treat them as our gods, and we fear that we may offend them. We take all our issues to them, asking them to pray for us because we believe they are our leaders and hear more from God. The Bible declares that we should honor our leaders, respect them, and pray for them. We are not to idolize them and replace God with them. We are supposed to seek God and spend more time with Him through prayer, worship and communicate consistently with Him to build that relationship that He so desires from us. Replacing God with our Pastors grieves the spirit of God, and in no time, God can break that relationship to draw us back to Him. Not surrendering fully to God can disrupt that loving, rich and intimate relationship with Him. When we accept Christ Jesus as our Lord and Personal Savior, we should surrender totally to Him. Most of the time, this is not so. We attend church services and participate in church programs, but then we are fully not surrendered to Him. We keep on holding to the ungodly things we were doing before coming to Him. This blocks us from fully receiving from God and developing that relationship with Him that will enable us to grow spiritually. Yielding fully to the Holy Spirit is beneficial since we tend to receive more from God and learn to know Him. For any relationship to develop fully, we need to spend time with each other to get to know ourselves. It is the same with Christ. Spending time with Him enables us to know His voice so we can discern when He talks to us.

Hypocrisy and pretense have become a norm among born-again believers. We do one thing in the church or among our fellow believers or when we are with our Pastors. When we go to work or other social gatherings, we exhibit another side because we just want to fit in. The Bible declares that those who are ashamed of Christ, He also will be ashamed of them and despise them (Luke 9:26). Many born-again believers go to parties, drink alcohol, misbehave, and pretend that behavior is acceptable. The hypocrisy is on another level these days. They return to church Sunday morning, taking the microphone and leading worship and service, pretending this is okay. How can you go in the presence of God with this attitude? The guilt alone keeps such a person from appearing before God. There are so many reasons why intimacy declines. It could be because of the ever-increasing busyness of life. Prayers are made for promotion, and when the promotion comes, we can no longer spend time in God's presence to pray and listen to Him. Our schedules become jam-packed with activities, sports, and office meetings too. Walk with the wise and you become wise. The Bible declares that iron sharpens iron (Proverbs 27:17). As we repent and accept Christ as our Lord and Savior, we should associate ourselves with those who know Christ and strive daily to walk according to His will. Often what makes us stray away is we continue to mingle with unbelievers, and gradually our walk with Christ becomes meaningless. When we engage in conversations that grieve the Holy Spirit that lives in us consistently, then the Spirit of the Lord gradually becomes nonexistent in our lives. We do not hear that gentle voice again, and we begin to do everything in our strength. By strength shall no man prevail (1 Samuel 2:9). Be very cautious as you develop this intimate relationship with Christ. Make sure you walk daily in constant communication through prayer and reading and studying the word. Avoid wrong company and never feel comfortable in any environment that will tempt you to sin against God. For instance, if you are invited to a party where they serve alcohol, you know alcohol is your weakest link. You could be easily tempted to fall back to your old ways, then either you decline the invitation, or you go and say a quick hello to the family and depart. Never take your relationship with Christ for granted and think you do not have to work hard to preserve it. He can quickly depart from you without you knowing. Rather, spend time with people in the same faith as you are, and you see them growing in their relationship with the Lord. Pray together, study the word together and strengthen each other through your faith journey. Be disciplined and stay away from sin as much as you can. Mark those who behave unruly among you and stay away from them (Romans 16:17-18).

A disobedient spirit will gradually break the relationship with God. Disobedience to God broke the relationship between Saul and God. God rejected Him and quickly replaced him with David because he disobeyed him. Never please any man and be loyal to man and disloyal to God.

God will definitely depart from you. Man will promise you, and the next minute break that promise but God will never fail you or leave you. Stick with God and maintain a deep and close relationship with Him for you to be able to fulfill your purpose here on earth. We can grieve the Holy Spirit or quench the spirit with sinful, corrupt, unkind words, obscene language, profanity, dirty stories, and vulgarity. Gossip grieves the Holy Spirit. Complaining and murmuring grieve His enabling power and His presence in our lives. Bitterness also grieves the Holy Spirit, and once the Holy Spirit is grieved, there is no connection or intimacy with Christ. Be assured the Holy Spirit lives inside you.

What you do in your life daily, you do to Him. Where you go every day, you take Him with you. When you go to the mall, He goes with you. What you look at online, He watches with you. When you choose to sin, you pull Him with you through that filth. Do you want to grieve Him? Of course not! So, decide today never to forget the Holy Spirit lives inside of you, and He deserves your utmost respect and honor in all you say and do. Several factors can block our ability to hear God. If not dealt with promptly, each can become a noise in our lives that stops us from discerning what the Lord is saying to us, thereby killing that intimate relationship with Christ. The most common and destructive of these factors is our self-will. We are so focused on our own needs and desires that we cannot hear what the Lord tells us. People influence our lives, and they will always have an opinion when we have a decision to make. But they are not you and will never know better than you what God's will is for your life. Another reason we may be hindered from a close relationship with the Lord is that we do not know God and His ways. We can be hindered from hearing God's will by fear in our hearts about our situation and doubt concerning the Lord's promises or character. How we feel about ourselves can hinder us from hearing God, especially if we see ourselves as unworthy of His love and concern. We all choose what we should do with our time, and often we may show that the Lord is our last priority by the small amount of time we spend with Him. We either consciously or unintentionally avoid knowing God's will because of unhealed anger and resentment we have toward Him. Harboring sin can hinder us from hearing God's will for our lives. When we go from sinning to harboring it, embracing, and shielding it as part of who we are and what we are entitled to, we put up a block between the Lord and us.

The greatest treasure apart from knowing Christ as our Personal Savior and having His Spirit indwelling in us is understanding God's purpose and plan for our lives. Do not allow any of the hindrances above to cause you to miss out on this awesome gift. Instead, pray often, asking God to evaluate you and do not ignore anything He reveals to you. Align yourself with Him and watch how His wonderful will unfold in your life.

PRAYERS THAT BRING INTIMACY WITH CHRIST JESUS

07

1. Father, draw me close to you in the Mighty Name of Jesus.

2. Father, connect me with the spiritual gift that will promote my life in the Mighty Name of Jesus.

3. I renounce every power of the flesh in the Mighty Name of Jesus.

4. Every arrow assigned to make me backslide backfire in the Mighty Name of Jesus.

5. Father, arise and order my steps in your word in the Mighty Name of Jesus.

6. Spiritual blindness and spiritual deafness, I reject you in the Mighty Name of Jesus.

7. Iniquity shall not have dominion over my life in the Mighty Name of Jesus.

8. Father, arise and open my eyes in the Mighty Name of Jesus.

9. Heavenly Father, create a longing within me for you in the

Mighty Name of Jesus.

10. Grace to seek first the Kingdom of God and His Righteousness; let it be my portion in the Mighty Name of Jesus.

11. Every unholy thing crippling in my life, I block you in the Mighty Name of Jesus.

12. I bind every spirit of slumber in the Mighty Name of Jesus.

13. Father, let the spirit to test and hunger for you fall upon my life in the Mighty Name of Jesus.

14. Forces of darkness pulling back my spiritual life depart in the Mighty Name of Jesus.

15. Powers assigned to attack my prayer life backfire in the Mighty Name of Jesus.

16. Every satanic power blocking my relationship with Christ, I bind you by the power in the blood of Jesus in the Mighty Name of Jesus.

17. I cast and bind every spirit of spiritual laziness in the Mighty Name of Jesus.

18. Any power assigned to reverse my spiritual progress go back to your senders in the Mighty Name of Jesus.

19. Baptism of the Holy Ghost Fire of God fall upon me

now in the Mighty Name of Jesus.

20. Heavenly Father, arise and bring my soul out of every satanic prison in the Mighty Name of Jesus.

21. Father, arise and revive my dead spiritual life in the Mighty Name of Jesus.

22. Anything that is slowing down my spiritual life be quickened by the fire of the Holy Ghost in the Mighty Name of Jesus.

23. Grace to spend daily quality time in your presence Lord, let it be my portion in the Mighty Name of Jesus.

24. Consistent prayer and fasting to seek your face, grant it unto me Lord in the Mighty Name of Jesus.

25. Meditation on the word of God daily, let it be my daily lifestyle in the Mighty Name of Jesus.

26. Power of the Holy Spirit overshadow my life in the Mighty Name of Jesus.

27. Spiritual visions, divine visitations, revelations, and encounters, let it be my portion in the Mighty Name of Jesus.

28. Heavenly Father, arise and endow me with the spirit of discernment in the Mighty Name of Jesus.

29. Father, arise and bestow unto me the yearning of a deep and abiding relationship with you in the Mighty Name of

Jesus.

30. The Presence of God overshadow my life in the Mighty Name of Jesus.

31. The Resurrection Power of the Lord Jesus Christ, come upon my life in the Mighty Name of Jesus.

32. Father, make me thirst for the Living Water in You in the Mighty Name of Jesus.

33. Father, help me love Jesus as You love Him that Your love for Jesus will be in me in the Mighty Name of Jesus.

34. Heavenly Father, give me the grace to love You more dearly, day by day, in the Mighty Name of Jesus.

35. I declare and decree that I will live for Jesus all my days in the Mighty Name of Jesus.

36. The enemy will not take me away from the presence of the Lord in the Mighty Name of Jesus.

37. Father Lord, baptize me with the spirit of wisdom and revelation to know you better in the Mighty Name of Jesus.

38. Father, create a longing within me for You in the Mighty Name of Jesus.

39. Father, increase the spirit of watchfulness and prayer in me in the Mighty Name of Jesus.

40. Grace to abide in your will and develop a rich and abiding relationship with you, grant it unto me in the Mighty Name of Jesus.

41. Father, let my daily declaration be *"All I want is Jesus"* in the Mighty Name of Jesus.

42. Father, let me know You and the Power of Your Resurrection in the Mighty Name of Jesus.

43. Father, let my soul and flesh thirst and long for you daily in the Mighty Name of Jesus.

44. Father, grant me the grace to know you intimately above everything else in the Mighty Name of Jesus.

45. Father, grant me the grace to be still before you daily in the Mighty Name of Jesus.

SCRIPTURES ON INTIMACY WITH CHRIST JESUS

08

- **Psalm 139:3-4 TPT**

You are so intimately aware of me, Lord. You read my heart like an open book, and you know all the words I am about to speak before I even start a sentence. You know every step I will take before my journey even begins.

- **Isaiah 43:10 TPT**

Yahweh says, "You are my witnesses, my chosen servants. I chose you in order that you would know me intimately, believe me always, and fully understand that I am the only God. There was no god before me, and there will be no other god after me.

- **Psalm 26:2-3 Voice**

Put me on trial and examine me, O Eternal One! Search me through and through - from my deepest longings to every thought that crosses my mind. Your unfailing love is always before me; I have journeyed down Your path of truth.

- **James 1:5 TPT**

"And if anyone longs to be wise, ask God for wisdom, and he will give it. He won't see your lack of wisdom as an opportunity to scold you over your failures, but he will overwhelm your failures with his generous

grace."

- **James 4:8 ESV**

Draw near to God, and he will draw near to you. Cleanse your hands, you sinners, and purify your hearts, you double-minded.

- **Jeremiah 29:11 ESV**

"For I know the plans I have for you," declares the Lord, "plans for welfare and not for evil, to give you a future and a hope."

- **Ephesians 1:17 NIV**

"I keep asking that the God of our Lord Jesus Christ, the glorious Father, may give you the Spirit of wisdom and revelation so that you may know him better."

- **Psalm 32:8 ESV**

"I will instruct you & teach you in the way you should go; I will counsel you with my eye upon you."

- **Psalm 16:11 NKJV**

"You will show me the path of life; In Your presence is fullness of joy; At Your right hand are pleasures forevermore."

- **Romans 8:28 NIV**

"And we know that in all things God works for the good of those who love him, who have been called according to his purpose."

- **2 Timothy 4:17 NIV**

"But the Lord stood at my side and gave me strength so that through me the message might be fully proclaimed and all the Gentiles might

hear it. And I was delivered from the lion's mouth."

- **Luke 12:21 NLT**

"Yes, a person is a fool to store up earthly wealth but not have a rich relationship with God."

- **Acts 17:28 NIV**

"For in him we live and move and have our being. As some of your own poets have said, we are his offspring."

- **Psalm 51:11 NIV**

"Do not cast me from your presence or take your Holy Spirit from me."

- **1 John 4:4 ESV**

"Little children, you are from God and have overcome them, for he who is in you is greater than he who is in the world."

- **Romans 8:31 KJV**

What shall we then say to these things? If God be for us, who can be against us?

- **Psalm 84:10 KJV**

For a day in thy courts is better than a thousand. I had rather be a doorkeeper in the house of my God than to dwell in the tents of wickedness.

- **Psalm 23:4 KJV**

Yea, though I walk through the valley of the shadow of death, I will fear no evil, for thou art with me; thy rod and thy staff they comfort *me.*

- **Philippians 3:8 (CEV)**

"Nothing is as wonderful as knowing Christ Jesus, my Lord. I have given up everything else and count it all as garbage. All I want is Christ."

- **Psalm 42:1-2 NIV**

"As a deer pants for flowing streams, so pants my soul for you, O God.
My soul thirsts for God, for the living God.
When shall I come and appear before God."

- **Job 22:23 KJV**

"If thou return to the Almighty, thou shalt be built up, thou shalt put away iniquity far from thy tabernacles."

- **Exodus 33:14 ESV**

"And He said, My Presence will go with you, and I will give you rest."

- **Psalm 73:25 ESV**

"Whom have I in heaven but you?
And there is nothing on earth that I desire besides you."

- **Psalm 139:7 ESV**

"Where shall I go from your Spirit?
Or where shall I flee from your presence?"

- **Isaiah 65:24 ESV**

"Before they call, I will answer; while they are yet speaking, I will hear."

- **Jeremiah 31:3 ESV**

The Lord appeared to him from far away. I have loved you with an everlasting love; therefore, I have continued my faithfulness to you.

- **Psalm 46:11 KJV**

The LORD of hosts is with us; the God of Jacob is our refuge.

- **Jeremiah 33:3 ESV**

"Call to me, and I will answer you and will tell you great and hidden things that you have not known."

- **1 Corinthians 10:31 ESV**

So, whether you eat or drink, or whatever you do, do all to the glory of God.

- **1 John 1:9 ESV**

If we confess our sins, he is faithful and just to forgive us our sins and to cleanse us from all unrighteousness.

- **1 Timothy 2:1 ESV**

First of all, then, I urge that supplications, prayers, intercessions, and thanksgivings be made for all people.

- **2 Corinthians 5:21 ESV**

For our sake, he made him to be sin who knew no sin, so that in him we might become the righteousness of God.

- **Colossians 3:1 ESV**

If then you have been raised with Christ, seek the things that are above, where Christ is, seated at the right hand of God.

- **Colossians 3:5 ESV**

Put to death, therefore, what is earthly in you: sexual immorality, impurity, passion, evil desire, and covetousness, which is idolatry.

- **Deuteronomy 6:5 ESV**

You shall love the Lord your God with all your heart and with all your soul and with all your might.

- **Genesis 1:27 ESV**

So God created man in his own image, in the image of God, he created him; male and female he created them.

- **Genesis 4:1 ESV**

Now Adam knew Eve, his wife, and she conceived and bore Cain, saying, "I have gotten a man with the help of the Lord."

- **Hebrews 11:6 ESV**

And without faith, it is impossible to please him, for whoever would draw near to God must believe that he exists and that he rewards those who seek him.

- **Isaiah 49:15 ESV**

"Can a woman forget her nursing child that she should have no compassion on the son of her womb? Even these may forget, yet I will not forget you."

- **Isaiah 55:7 ESV**

Let the wicked forsake his way, and the unrighteous man his thoughts; let him return to the Lord, that he may have compassion on him, and to our God, for he will abundantly pardon.

- **John 15:15 ESV**

"No longer do I call you servants, for the servant, does not know what his master is doing, but I have called you friends, for all that I have heard from my Father I have made known to you."

- **John 17:3 ESV**

"And this is eternal life, that they know you the only true God, and Jesus Christ whom you have sent."

- **John 3:16 ESV**

For God so loved the world, that he gave his only Son, that whoever believes in him should not perish but have eternal life.

- **Joshua 1:9 ESV**

"Have I not commanded you? Be strong and courageous. Do not be frightened, and do not be dismayed, for the Lord your God is with you wherever you go."

- **Philippians 3:10 ESV**

That I may know him and the power of his resurrection, and may share his sufferings, becoming like him in his death.

- **Psalm 46:10 ESV**

"Be still and know that I am God. I will be exalted among the nations, I will be exalted in the earth!"

- **Revelation 3:20 ESV**

"Behold, I stand at the door and knock. If anyone hears my voice and opens the door, I will come into him and eat with him, and he with me."

- **Romans 5:8 ESV**

But God shows his love for us in that while we were still sinners, Christ died for us.

- **Song of Solomon 2:10 ESV**

My beloved speaks and says to me: "Arise, my love, my beautiful one, and come away."

- **Zephaniah 3:17 ESV**

The Lord your God is in your midst, a mighty one who will save; he will rejoice over you with gladness; he will quiet you by his love; he will exult over you with loud singing.

- **Acts 10:38 ESV**

How God anointed Jesus of Nazareth with the Holy Ghost and with power: who went about doing good and healing all that were oppressed of the devil; for God was with him.

- **Hebrews 13:5 KJV**

Let your conversation be without covetousness; and be content with such things as ye have: for he hath said, I will never leave thee, nor forsake thee.

- **Isaiah 41:10 NIV**

So do not fear, for I am with you; do not be dismayed, for I am your God.
I will strengthen you and help you;
I will uphold you with my righteous right hand.

- **Isaiah 43:1 NIV**

But now, this is what the LORD says —
he who created you, Jacob,
he who formed you, Israel:
"Do not fear, for I have redeemed you;
I have summoned you by name; you are mine.

- **Isaiah 43:4-5 NIV**

Since you are precious and honored in my sight, and because I love you,
I will give people in exchange for you, nations in exchange for your life.
Do not be afraid, for I am with you; I will bring your children from the east and gather you from the west.

- **Hosea 2:19-20 NIV**

I will betroth you to me forever; I will betroth you in righteousness and justice, in love and compassion.
I will betroth you in faithfulness, and you will acknowledge the LORD.

- **Jeremiah 3:14 NIV**

Return, faithless people," declares the LORD, "for I am your husband. I will choose you— one from a town and two from a clan— and bring you to Zion.

- **Jeremiah 9:24 NIV**

But let the one who boasts boast about this: that they have the understanding to know me, that I am the LORD, who exercises kindness, justice and righteousness on earth; for in these I delight," declares the LORD

- **Genesis 1:26a NIV**

Then God said, "Let us make mankind in our image, in our likeness…

- **Psalm 34:10 NLT**

Even strong young lions sometimes go hungry, but those who trust in the LORD will lack no good thing.

- **Hosea 6:3 ESV**

Let us know; let us press on to know the LORD;
 his going out is sure as the dawn;
he will come to us as the showers, as the spring rains that water the earth."

CONNECT AND STAY WITH JESUS — 09

God has a plan and purpose for your life. Accepting Jesus as your Lord and Personal Savior and getting to know Him intimately is the beginning of a fulfilling life and destiny.

My prayer is as you get a copy of this book and you read it, you will take the necessary steps to begin an intimate relationship with Jesus. This will completely transform your life and mindset. Stay in the word daily by reading your Bible and meditating on it. *"This book of the law shall not depart out of thy mouth; but thou shalt meditate therein day and night, that thou mayest observe to do according to all that is written therein: for then thou shall make thy way prosperous, and then thou shall have good success."* Joshua 1:8 (KJV).

Be committed to a lifestyle of prayer. Pray ALWAYS! *"Never stop praying"* 1 Thessalonians 5:17 (NLT). Prayer will keep you in constant communication with God. Talk to Him about everything, anywhere, and anytime. He is Omnipresent and with you always. Through the prayers, the Lord will speak to you and order your steps so you can walk in the perfect will of God for your life. Be sensitive to the Holy Spirit and let the Spirit of the Lord always lead you. *"But when the Father sends the Advocate as my representative - that is, the Holy Spirit - he will teach you everything and will remind you of everything I have told you."* John 14:26 (NLT). The rationale behind this book is for you to fulfill your purpose here on earth while enjoying a loving, rich, intimate, and abiding relationship with Christ Jesus. Tell the world about Jesus in your own small way. Raise the banner of His Name until the Nations call on Him. This is a direct instruction from the Bible. *"Go into all the world and preach the gospel to all creation."* Mark 16:15 (NIV).

My heart has found great peace through my relationship with God, and it has transformed my life in ways I never even dreamed were possible. Share your love with God today and let him into your heart. In this way, you can experience the beauty and benefits of your divine relationship with God, our Creator, for yourself. After your encounter with this book, my prayer for you is that you will make Heaven, and your name will appear in the Book of Life. Let the Holy Spirit minister to you as you read.

SALVATION PRAYER — 10

Heavenly Father, I come to You admitting that I am a sinner (Romans 3:23)

Right now, I choose to turn away from my sins and I ask You to cleanse me by Your blood, of all unrighteousness. I believe that Your Son, Jesus, died on the cross to take away my sins.

I also believe that He rose again from the dead so that I may be justified and made righteous through faith in Him (Romans 6:23). I call upon the name of Jesus Christ to be the Savior and Lord of my life (Acts 2:21).

I declare right now that I am a born-again child of God (Romans 10:9-10). I am free from sin, and full of the righteousness of God. I am saved in Jesus Name. I choose to follow You and I ask that You fill me with the Power of the Holy Spirit (Luke 11:3) in Jesus Mighty Name, Amen.

Pleasant Reading. God bless you immensely!

ABOUT THE AUTHOR

Susie Adwoa Koffie is a Woman of God who loves the Lord passionately. She is the host of the Midnight Hour Prayer-Line that is operated via telephone every midnight. This is her first book written by the leading of the Holy Spirit. Her hope is that everyone who comes in contact with this book will develop a very loving, rich, deep, abiding and intimate relationship with Christ Jesus making them Heaven bound.

"Come close to God, and God will come close to you" James 4:8 (NLT).

My Daily Walk with God
Journal Notes

"Come close to God, and God will come close to you"

James 4:8 (NLT)

How can I develop a more intimate relationship with God?:

What steps can I take to get closer to God?:

People I am Interceding for:

(I am committing to praying for these people this year)

1. _____
2. _____
3. _____
4. _____
5. _____
6. _____
7. _____
8. _____
9. _____
10. _____

Ministries, Pastors, Countries, etc. I am Interceding for:

1. _____
2. _____
3. _____
4. _____
5. _____
6. _____
7. _____
8. _____
9. _____
10. _____

Situations I am praying about this year:

1. _____
2. _____
3. _____
4. _____
5. _____
6. _____
7. _____
8. _____
9. _____
10. _____

Reflection

Study Notes

Susie Adwoa Koffie